Le PICNIC

Le PICNIC

Chic food for on-the-go

SUZY ASHFORD

Smith
Street
Books

CONTENTS

INTRODUCTION

When the sun is shining and the sky is sparkling blue, it would be remiss to lunch indoors – especially in those first bursts of spring after a long winter. Take advantage of the warm air and sunshine by eating outdoors.

A picnic can be as simple as a packaged sandwich and a coffee on a patch of grass or a park chair – but put in a little effort, and it can be more chic than a Chanel suit on the Champs-Élysées.

Le Picnic re-imagines outdoor eating as an elegant, delightful and delicious activity to enjoy with friends. All the recipes in this book are designed for sharing – from the dips and terrines, to the larger tarts, baguettes, salads and sweet treats. Of course, having more friends at your picnic means more of the delicious recipes to make and share – so get those invites out!

As you would expect from a picnic book, many of the recipes can be made a day or so ahead, but all are able to be transported to your chosen destination – whether that be Paris's Luxembourg Gardens or your own backyard.

And since we're putting so much effort into getting the menu just right, let's think beyond plastic cutlery, paper plates and cheap napkins. Equally, if you're bringing along a bottle of bubbles (a vital element to any picnic), serving it in a coffee mug or plastic tumbler just isn't going to cut it – only a glass coupe or flute will do. Cheers – and bon appétit!

Le SNACK

baked
SAVOURY FIGS

8 fresh figs

60 g (2 oz) goat's cheese, cut into 8 portions

8 walnut halves, roughly chopped

sea salt flakes

pomegranate syrup, for drizzling

Preheat the oven to 160°C/320°F (fan-forced). Line a baking tray with baking paper and place the figs on it, sitting upright.

Cut a cross into the top of each fig and fill with the cheese and walnuts. Add a sprinkling of salt and a few drops of pomegranate syrup. Bake for 10 minutes. Serve warm, or transfer to an airtight container for transporting and enjoy at room temperature.

These delicious figs are perfect for a pre-lunch nibble or as part of a platter with charcuterie, olives, pickled vegetables and cheeses, or with Salmon rillettes (see page 22) and baguette slices.

Makes 8

NOTE
To make the gougères well ahead of time, freeze the unbaked dough when you have piped or spooned it onto the baking trays. On the day of your picnic, remove from the freezer and bake as directed.

gougères
CHEESE PUFFS

40 g (1½ oz) butter

75 g (2¾ oz/½ cup) plain (all-purpose) flour

pinch of smoked paprika

¼ teaspoon sea salt

2 extra-large free-range eggs

60 g (2 oz/½ cup) grated cheddar

60 g (2 oz/½ cup) grated gruyère

Preheat the oven to 180°C/350°F (fan-forced). Line two baking trays with baking paper.

Place the butter and 125 ml (4 fl oz/½ cup) water in a small heavy-based saucepan over medium heat. Bring to the boil, add the flour, paprika and salt and stir with a wooden spoon for 1–2 minutes, until the mixture leaves the side of the pan and forms a ball.

Transfer the mixture to the bowl of an electric mixer and allow to cool for 2 minutes. Add the eggs one at a time, beating well after each addition. Combine the two cheeses and add three-quarters of the mixture to the bowl, stirring through until combined. The finished pastry should be firm and glossy.

Spoon the mixture into a piping (icing) bag, then pipe even-sized balls onto the lined baking trays, or spoon tablespoons of the mixture onto the baking trays, allowing space in between for rising. Sprinkle with the remaining cheese mixture and bake for 10 minutes.

Reduce the oven temperature to 160°C/320°F (fan-forced) and cook for a further 15 minutes, or until golden and hollow. Cool slightly on the trays.

Transfer to an airtight container for transporting. The gougères are best enjoyed the day they are made, but can be baked the day before, stored in the fridge, and brought to room temperature for serving.

Makes 15

pistachio, lemon thyme
& CHICKEN TERRINE

200 g (7 oz) thinly sliced
  prosciutto

1 tablespoon olive oil

1 onion, finely chopped

2 garlic cloves, crushed

1 kg (2 lb 3 oz) boneless,
  skinless chicken thighs,
  fat trimmed

50 g (1¾ oz/⅓ cup)
  pistachio nuts

1 tablespoon lemon thyme
  leaves

1 tablespoon chopped flat-
  leaf (Italian) parsley

finely grated zest of
  ½ orange

1 teaspoon sea salt flakes

60 ml (2 fl oz/½ cup) brandy

2 free-range egg yolks,
  lightly beaten

baguette, to serve

cornichons, to serve

Preheat the oven to 150°C/300°F (fan-forced). Lightly grease a 1.2 litre (41 fl oz) loaf (bar) tin, measuring about 20 cm x 10 cm (8 inches x 4 inches).

Line the tin with rows of the prosciutto, overlapping each slice slightly and leaving enough prosciutto hanging over the sides of the tin to wrap back over and enclose the top of the terrine. Each row will need 2 slices of prosciutto, slightly overlapping end to end. Chop up any remaining prosciutto.

Heat the olive oil in a frying pan and add the onion, garlic and chopped prosciutto. Cook over medium heat, stirring occasionally, for 4–5 minutes, or until the onion is tender. Remove from the heat and set aside to cool.

Meanwhile, working in two batches, place the chicken in a food processor and pulse until roughly chopped. Do not over-process: it is desirable to have a variable texture in the chicken. Transfer the chopped chicken to a large bowl and stir in the pistachios, herbs, orange zest, salt, brandy, egg yolks and sautéed onion mixture. Mix well.

Transfer the mixture to the prosciutto-lined loaf tin, pressing down firmly. Smooth the top and fold the overhanging prosciutto over the top of the mixture. Cover with foil.

Place the terrine in a large, deep roasting tin and fill the tin with enough hot water to come halfway up the sides of the loaf tin. Bake for 1¼ hours, or until the terrine is firm when pressed, and the internal temperature has reached 75°C/170°F.

Remove the terrine from the oven and carefully pour out and discard any liquid. Place the terrine on a tray and weigh it down with several tins of food, or a brick covered in foil, to compress the terrine. Refrigerate overnight.

Serve sliced, with baguette and cornichons.

This terrine will keep in the fridge for up to 4 days.

Serves 12

NOTE
Quiche Lorraine does not traditionally contain cheese, but the gruyère adds a bit of 'oomph' to these mini quiches. You can leave it out if you like.

mini quiche
LORRAINES

200 g (7 oz) bacon, cut into thin strips

60 g (2 oz/½ cup) grated gruyère (optional)

4 free-range eggs

125 ml (4 fl oz/½ cup) pouring (single/light) cream (35% fat)

pinch of freshly grated nutmeg

SHORTCRUST PASTRY

225 g (8 oz/1½ cups) plain (all-purpose) flour

125 g (4½ oz) cold butter, chopped

1 egg yolk

1 tablespoon iced water, approximately

To make the pastry, place the flour and butter in a food processor and pulse until the mixture resembles breadcrumbs. Add the egg yolk and water and process until the ingredients just come together, adding a little more water if necessary. Press the dough into a flat disc shape, cover with plastic wrap and refrigerate for 30 minutes.

Roll out the pastry between two sheets of baking paper as thinly as you can (2–3 mm/$\frac{1}{16}$–$\frac{1}{8}$ inch thick), then cut out 18 rounds using an 8.5 cm (3¼ inch) cutter. Use the pastry rounds to line 18 muffin holes, each 80 ml (2½ fl oz/ ⅓ cup) in capacity. The pastry will not come all the way up the sides of each muffin hole; the quiches will be quite shallow.

Preheat the oven to 160°C/320°F (fan-forced). Meanwhile, place the pastry back in the fridge to rest while the oven is heating.

Sauté the bacon in a non-stick frying pan over medium heat until cooked through and lightly browned. Drain on paper towel.

Divide the bacon evenly among the pastry cases. Top with a sprinkling of gruyère, if using. Whisk the eggs, cream, nutmeg and some sea salt and freshly ground black pepper together in a jug, then carefully pour over the bacon and cheese. Do not over-fill the pastry cases.

Bake for 15–20 minutes, or until the pastry is browned and cooked through and the filling is puffed and golden. Cool for 5 minutes in the tins, before transferring to a wire rack to cool completely.

These quiches are lovely served still slightly warm. They can also be made a day ahead and refrigerated in an airtight container until needed; bring back to room temperature for serving.

Makes 18

chicken liver
<u>PÂTÉ</u>

500 g (1 lb 2 oz) chicken livers, trimmed

150 g (5½ oz) butter, chopped and softened

8 sage leaves

2 French shallots, finely chopped

80 ml (2½ fl oz/⅓ cup) brandy

freshly ground white pepper

FOR COVERING THE PÂTÉ
80 g (2¾ oz) unsalted butter, chopped

4 sage leaves

Place the chicken livers in a colander, rinse gently under cold water and drain. Pat dry with paper towel.

Heat about a tablespoon of the softened butter and 4 of the sage leaves in a heavy-based frying pan over medium–high heat until the butter melts and foams. Working in two batches, add the livers to the pan and cook for 3–5 minutes, or until lightly browned on the outside and slightly pink on the inside. Transfer the livers to a plate.

Add the shallot and remaining sage leaves to the frying pan and cook over medium–low heat, stirring occasionally, for 5 minutes, or until the shallot is soft, adding a little more of the butter to the pan if needed.

Return the livers to the pan and add the brandy. Carefully ignite the brandy if you like. Simmer for 1 minute, or until the liquid has almost evaporated. Remove and discard the sage leaves. Leave to cool slightly.

Place the liver mixture in a food processor and blend until smooth, scraping down the side of the bowl if necessary. Working in batches, transfer the mixture to a coarse-mesh sieve set over a bowl, and use a metal spoon to rub and push the mixture through the sieve.

Return the sieved liver mixture to the food processor with the remaining softened butter. Process, scraping down the side of the bowl as needed, until the mixture is smooth and well combined. Taste and season with salt and white pepper.

Spoon the pâté mixture into a 400 ml (14 fl oz) dish (or several smaller dishes) and smooth the surface. Set aside.

Place the unsalted butter and sage leaves in a small saucepan and place over medium heat until it just melts. Pour the clarified butter evenly over the surface of the pâté, leaving the white milk solids behind. Arrange the sage leaves on top. Once the butter sets, cover the pâté with plastic wrap and refrigerate overnight to set and develop the flavours. This pâté will keep in the fridge for up to 5 days.

Serve with fresh or toasted thinly sliced baguette, crackers, or with slices of pear.

Serves 6–8; makes about 375 g (13 oz/1½ cups)

NOTE
The pastry for these tartlets
is lovely and pliable to work
with, and crumbly and
delicious to eat! Instead of
making six tartlets, you could
make five slightly larger
ones, using 10 cm (4 inch)
tart tins.

tomato
TARTLETS

3 teaspoons dijon mustard, or more to taste

24 cherry tomatoes, cut into thirds, or 6 thick tomato slices (about 7–8 cm/2¾–3¼ inches in diameter)

3 teaspoons thyme leaves

60 g (2 oz) goat's cheese, crumbled

extra virgin olive oil, for drizzling

PASTRY

225 g (8 oz/1½ cups) plain (all-purpose) flour, plus extra for dusting

½ teaspoon sea salt

125 g (4½ oz) unsalted butter, chilled and cut into small cubes

1 extra-large free-range egg

To make the pastry, combine the flour and salt on a work surface or in a large shallow bowl. Rub in the butter until the mixture resembles large, coarse crumbs. Make a well in the centre.

Crack the egg into a small bowl, beat in 2 tablespoons water, then add to the flour mixture and stir it through until the mixture comes together to form a soft dough. Add another 2 teaspoons water if required to bring the dough together.

Roll the pastry out on a lightly floured surface, to fit six 8 cm (3¼ inch) loose-based tart (flan) tins. Ease the pastry into the tins, gently pressing into the side of each tin, then trimming the pastry edges. Prick the bases and chill in the fridge for 20 minutes while preparing the other ingredients.

Preheat the oven to 180°C/350°F (fan-forced).

Spread each pastry case with about ½ teaspoon mustard, or a little more if you prefer. Over the mustard, arrange 12 cherry tomato slices, quite close together, or a thick slice of tomato. Sprinkle each with ½ teaspoon thyme, then scatter over the goat's cheese. Drizzle with a little olive oil and season with sea salt and freshly ground black pepper.

Bake for 20–25 minutes, or until the pastry is golden. Allow to cool for 5 minutes before removing from the tart tins.

These tartlets are wonderful enjoyed just warm, within a few hours of baking, with salad. They will keep in an airtight container in the fridge for a few days; bring to room temperature for serving.

Makes 6

salmon
__RILLETTES__

200 ml (7 fl oz) dry white wine

½ French shallot, thickly sliced

250 g (9 oz) salmon fillet

sea salt flakes

100 g (3½ oz) smoked salmon, finely chopped, reserving a piece to garnish

3 dill sprigs, stems removed, plus an extra sprig to garnish

1 tablespoon lemon juice

125 g (4½ oz/½ cup) crème fraîche or light sour cream

In a small saucepan, bring the wine, shallot and 250 ml (8½ fl oz/1 cup) water to the boil over medium heat. Season the salmon fillet with salt and add it to the hot liquid. Simmer for 2 minutes, then remove from the heat and leave to rest in the poaching liquid for 10 minutes.

Using a slotted spoon, remove the salmon from the poaching liquid and place in a mixing bowl. Cover and leave until cool. Remove the skin and any bones, then flake the salmon. Add the smoked salmon, dill, lemon juice and crème fraîche and stir with a spatula until combined.

Pack the rillettes into a serving bowl and garnish with the reserved smoked salmon and dill. Cover and chill until needed; the rillettes will keep for 3 days.

To serve, spread onto fresh baguette or cucumber slices, or spread into lengths of celery.

Serves 8–10 as a starter

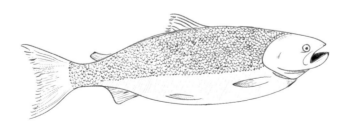

NOTE
The duck fat from the confit can be strained, cooled, poured into a clean airtight container and reused. It will keep for up to 6 weeks in the fridge, or up to 3 months in the freezer.

duck confit & cherry
MINI CROUSTADES

FOR THE DUCK

1 French shallot, finely chopped

3 garlic cloves, crushed

3 thyme sprigs

3 tablespoons sea salt flakes

4 duck leg quarters

1 litre (34 fl oz/4 cups) duck or goose fat

FOR THE CROUSTADE

1 tablespoon olive oil

1 large French shallot, thinly sliced

¼ red cabbage, finely shaved

1 fennel bulb, shaved

2 teaspoons apple cider vinegar

200 g (7 oz/1 cup) fresh or frozen cherries, pitted

125 ml (4 fl oz/½ cup) melted butter

12 filo pastry sheets

Prepare the duck a day ahead. Combine the shallot, garlic, thyme, salt and some freshly ground black pepper in a mixing bowl. Coat the duck pieces in the mixture and place in a zip-lock bag. Refrigerate for 24 hours.

Preheat the oven to 150°C/300°F (fan-forced). Rinse the salt mixture from the duck skin, then pat dry. Pack the pieces snugly, in a single layer, in a small high-sided ovenproof dish.

Melt the duck fat in a small saucepan and pour it over the duck pieces, ensuring they are completely submerged. Place the ovenproof dish in the oven and cook for 2½ hours, or until the duck is tender and comes easily off the bone. Remove from the oven and allow to cool. Remove the duck from the fat, shred the meat and skin, and discard the bones.

To make the croustades, heat the olive oil in a frying pan over medium heat and add the shallot. Cook, stirring, for 4 minutes, or until softened. Add the cabbage and cook for 10 minutes, or until it is tender and the liquid has reduced. Now add the fennel and cook for a further 4–5 minutes. Mix in the cherries and duck meat and cook for a few minutes further to warm through.

Preheat the oven to 180°C/350°F (fan-forced). Brush the cups of a large 12-hole muffin tin with melted butter.

Lay a filo sheet out on a work surface and brush with melted butter. Repeat with five more layers. Keep the remaining pastry under a clean dry tea towel, so the sheets don't dry out. Cut the filo rectangle into six squares, about 12 cm (5 inches) in size. Repeat with the remaining filo sheets. Line the muffin holes with the pastry.

Use tongs to partly fill the pastry cups with the duck mixture, allowing enough room to fold the pastry edges over and enclose the filling. Brush the tops with more melted butter to seal.

Bake for 15 minutes, or until the pastry is golden. Serve warm, or leave to cool, then refrigerate in an airtight container for transporting, and serve at room temperature.

Makes 12

pork & pistachio
__TERRINE__

700 g (1 lb 9 oz) pork, minced (ground) coarsely

300 g (10½ oz) pork fat, minced (ground) coarsely

75 g (2¾ oz/½ cup) pistachio nuts, roughly chopped

3 tablespoons Cognac

½ teaspoon freshly ground white pepper

¼ teaspoon ground nutmeg

¼ teaspoon ground cloves

¼ teaspoon ground cinnamon

3 teaspoons sea salt flakes

25 g (1 oz/¾ cup) chopped flat-leaf (Italian) parsley

3 tablespoons chopped chervil

In a mixing bowl, combine the pork, pork fat, pistachios, Cognac, spices and salt. Mix together well, then cover and refrigerate overnight to marinate.

The next day, preheat the oven to 180°C/350°F (fan-forced).

Add the parsley and chervil to the pork mixture and mix well. Transfer the mixture to a 30 cm (12 inch) terrine mould (1 litre/34 fl oz/4 cup capacity), pressing down firmly. Smooth the top, cover with foil, then place the terrine in a large, deep roasting tin.

Pour boiling water into the roasting tin, to come halfway up the sides of the terrine mould. Transfer to the oven and bake for 1 hour.

Remove the terrine from the oven, remove the foil cover, and allow to cool for 1 hour. Cover with baking paper, then place a weight on top, such as a large, square bottle of olive oil, to compress the terrine. Refrigerate overnight.

Cut the terrine into slices and serve as part of a cold platter, or in a baguette.

Serves 6–8

NOTE
Begin the terrine two days
in advance, as it requires
one day to marinate and
another day to chill.

herb & roasted garlic
GOAT'S CHEESE

1 whole garlic bulb

1 teaspoon olive oil

sea salt flakes and freshly
ground white pepper,
to taste

200 g (7 oz) soft marinated
goat's cheese

100 g (3½ oz) cream
cheese, softened

3 tablespoons chopped
herbs, such as flat-leaf
(Italian) parsley, tarragon
and chives

Preheat the oven to 180°C/350°F (fan-forced).

Remove any loose papery skin from the outside of the garlic bulb, then trim
off the top 5 mm (¼ inch) of the bulb, leaving the bulb intact. Place the garlic
bulb on a square of foil, cut side up, drizzle the olive oil over the cut surface and
sprinkle with sea salt flakes. Wrap the foil around the garlic and place it directly
on an oven rack. Roast for 35–40 minutes, or until soft. Remove from the oven
and set aside to cool.

Squeeze the roasted garlic cloves out of their skins and place in a food
processor. Add the remaining ingredients and blend until smooth, scraping down
the side of the bowl if necessary. Taste and season with sea salt flakes and
freshly ground white pepper.

Transfer to a small airtight container and refrigerate until required. This cheese
will keep in the fridge for up to 7 days.

Serve with baguette slices and baby vegetables.

Makes about 300 g (10½ oz/1¼ cups)

caramelised onion &
GOAT'S CHEESE TARTLETS

60 ml (2 fl oz/¼ cup) olive oil

4 large red onions, thinly
sliced

pinch of sea salt flakes

1 rosemary sprig

1 tablespoon balsamic
vinegar

2 teaspoons soft brown
sugar

200 g (7 oz) goat's cheese

SHORTCRUST PASTRY
(*PÂTE* BRISÉE)

240 g (8½ oz/scant
1⅔ cups) plain (all-
purpose) flour, plus extra
for dusting

180 g (6½ oz) cold butter,
cut into 5 mm (¼ inch)
cubes

60 ml (2 fl oz/¼ cup) chilled
water

melted butter, for brushing

Heat the olive oil in a heavy-based saucepan over medium heat, then add the onion and salt. Stir to coat the onion with the oil, then cover and cook for 10–15 minutes, or until the onion has softened, stirring occasionally. Add the rosemary sprig and turn the heat down to low. Cover and continue to cook, stirring occasionally, for a further 30 minutes. Stir in the vinegar and sugar and cook for a further 10 minutes, or until the onion becomes a rich caramel brown.

While the onion is caramelising, make the pastry. Sift the flour onto a clean work surface. Toss the butter cubes in the flour, then rub in lightly; pieces of butter should still be visible. Make a well in the centre and pour in the water. Working quickly, combine the mixture into a rough paste. Use the back of your hand to smear the pastry away from you, to further combine the butter with the flour.

Gather the pastry together and form into a thick, flat disc. Wrap in plastic wrap and refrigerate for 30 minutes.

When you're ready to make the tartlets, generously dust your work surface with flour, and brush four 10 cm (4 inch) tart (flan) tins with melted butter. Roll out the chilled pastry to a 5 mm (¼ inch) thickness. Cut out four circles a little larger than the tart tins, allowing a little extra up the sides as the pastry will shrink during baking. Line the tins with the pastry, pressing gently into the edges of the tins.

Chill the pastry in the tins for 20 minutes. Meanwhile, preheat the oven to 200°C/400°F (fan-forced).

Carefully line the pastry cases with baking paper and fill with baking beads, dried beans or rice. Bake for 15 minutes, then remove the paper and weights and bake for a further 5 minutes.

Put the caramelised onion in a mixing bowl. Crumble the goat's cheese in, then stir gently to just combine. Divide the mixture among the pastry cases and bake for 12 minutes.

Serve warm or at room temperature, with green salad leaves. These tartlets are best eaten the day they are made.

Serves 4

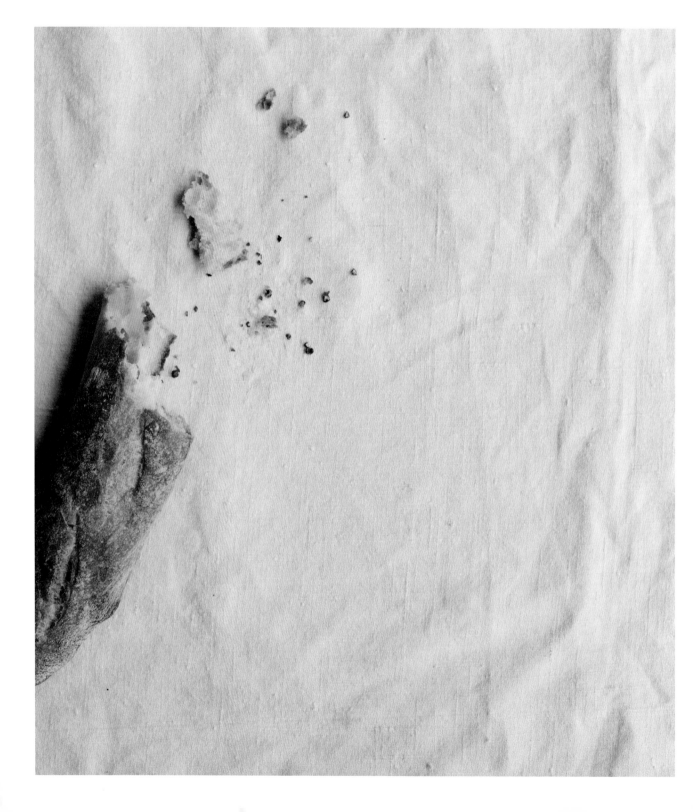

FOOD FOR SHARING

watercress, egg &
JAMBON BAGUETTE

1 teaspoon white vinegar

6 free-range eggs

3 tablespoons homemade or good-quality mayonnaise

2 tablespoons wholegrain mustard

3 tablespoons chopped chives

4 cornichons, finely chopped

1 large baguette

160 g (5½ oz) sliced jambon or leg ham

2 large handfuls picked watercress

Bring a small saucepan of water to the boil and add the vinegar. Gently lower the eggs into the boiling water and simmer for 8 minutes. Remove the eggs from the pan with a slotted spoon and refresh in an ice bath or in cold water until cool enough to handle.

Peel the eggs and place in a bowl. Mash with a fork until roughly broken up. Add the mayonnaise, mustard, chives and cornichons and stir gently until just combined. Season with sea salt and freshly ground black pepper to taste.

Using a large serrated knife, cut the baguette in half horizontally, leaving the back edge of the crust intact. Spread the egg mixture over the base of the baguette, then top with the ham and watercress.

Close the baguette back together and cut into four portions. Wrap each portion securely in baking paper for transportation.

Keep chilled until ready to serve. The baguettes are best enjoyed the day they are made.

Serves 4

olive & anchovy
PISSALADIÈRE

2 tablespoons olive oil (or oil from the anchovy fillets, below)

5 onions, halved and thinly sliced

1 thyme sprig

1 flat-leaf (Italian) parsley sprig

1 bay leaf

2 garlic cloves, peeled and bruised, but left whole

1 tablespoon capers, drained and rinsed

50 g (1¾ oz) good-quality anchovy fillets (about 20), drained

12 niçoise or other black olives, pitted

FOR THE DOUGH

300 g (10½ oz/2 cups) strong flour or plain (all-purpose) flour, plus extra for dusting

1 teaspoon active dried yeast

¾ teaspoon fine salt

1 tablespoon olive oil

To make the dough, combine the flour, yeast and salt in a large bowl. Make a well in the centre, then pour in the olive oil and 200 ml (7 fl oz) warm water and mix until combined. Cover the bowl with plastic wrap and set aside for 10 minutes.

Turn the dough out onto a lightly floured work surface and knead for 4–5 minutes, until quite smooth and elastic. Place in a lightly oiled bowl, cover with plastic wrap and set aside in a warm place for about 1 hour, or until doubled in size.

While the dough is rising, caramelise the onion. Heat the olive oil in a large heavy-based frying pan over medium–low heat. Add the onion, thyme, parsley, bay leaf and garlic. Cook, stirring often, for 50–60 minutes, or until the onion is meltingly soft and slightly golden. Remove and discard the herb sprigs, bay leaf and garlic.

Chop the capers and 6 of the anchovy fillets together. Mix them into the caramelised onion and season generously with freshly ground black pepper, and a little sea salt if required. Set aside until needed.

Preheat the oven to 200°C/400°F (fan-forced).

On a lightly floured work surface, gently roll and stretch the dough out to a 30 cm x 25 cm (12 inch x 10 inch) rectangle. Place on a large baking tray lined with baking paper.

Gently spread the onion mixture over the dough, leaving a 1.5 cm (½ inch) border around the edge. Bake for 20 minutes, or until the dough is golden and nearly cooked through.

Remove from the oven and top with the remaining anchovy fillets and olives, in a decorative criss-cross pattern. Bake for a further 5 minutes, or until the dough base is cooked.

The pissaladière is best eaten on the day it is made.

Serves 6–8

lamb &
POTATO PIES

500 g (1 lb 2 oz) boneless
   lamb shoulder, trimmed
   of fat, cut into 2 cm
   (¾ inch) cubes

2 tablespoons olive oil

4 brown onions, thinly sliced

2 garlic cloves, crushed

1 rosemary sprig, finely
   chopped

125 ml (4 fl oz/½ cup) dry
   white wine

500 ml (17 fl oz/2 cups)
   chicken stock

melted butter, for brushing

6 potatoes, peeled and very
   thinly sliced

Season the lamb with sea salt and freshly ground black pepper. Heat the olive oil in a large saucepan over medium–high heat. Cooking in batches to avoid overcrowding the pan, brown the lamb well, for 8–10 minutes each batch, adding more oil if necessary. Remove the lamb from the pan.

Reduce the heat to medium–low, add the onion to the pan and cook for 10 minutes, or until softened and golden, stirring to scrape up any brown bits on the base of the pan. Add the garlic and cook for a further minute or two.

Return the lamb to the pan. Stir in the rosemary and wine, then cook for a few minutes, until the wine has evaporated.

Stir in the stock, then cover and simmer for 1–1¼ hours, or until the meat is tender and the liquid has reduced and thickened. At this point you can continue on to make the pies, or chill the mixture overnight in the fridge; the next day, skim off any fat from the top of the lamb mixture.

When you're ready to bake the pies, preheat the oven to 150°C/300°F (fan-forced).

Brush four 300 ml (10 fl oz) capacity ramekins with melted butter. Line the base of each ramekin with potato slices, then spoon in the lamb mixture. Top with the remaining potatoes, arranging the slices to overlap and cover the filling. Cut out circles of baking paper to fit the ramekins. Brush the paper rounds with melted butter, place buttered side down onto the top of the pies, then press down gently.

Place the ramekins on a baking tray, then into the oven. Bake for 1 hour.

Remove the baking paper 'lids' and continue to bake for a further 20–30 minutes, or until the potato slices are golden brown.

Serve warm or at room temperature, with a green salad.

Serves 4

roast chicken &
CAMEMBERT BAGUETTE

½ cold roast chicken

1 large fresh crusty baguette

250 g (9 oz) camembert, thickly sliced

2–3 handfuls mesclun salad leaves

2 tablespoons good-quality mayonnaise

4 cornichons, chopped

1 tablespoon capers, chopped

½ small red onion, finely chopped

1 tablespoon chopped flat-leaf (Italian) parsley

Remove the bones and fatty bits from the roast chicken. Slice the flesh and set aside.

Use a serrated knife to slice the baguette horizontally from end to end, but not all the way through — keeping it hinged, if possible, will help in handling.

Place the cheese slices evenly along the base of the baguette. Top with the salad leaves, pressing them down firmly and gently, then place the chicken slices on top.

In a small bowl, combine the mayonnaise, cornichons, capers, onion and parsley, and spread the mixture inside the lid of the baguette.

Cut into four or six portions, then wrap each one in greaseproof paper (you could also use baking paper, although it is stiffer and won't be as easy to handle). Tie with kitchen string or raffia.

Keep in the fridge and transport to your picnic destination in a chilled container. The baguettes are best enjoyed on the day of making.

Serves 4–6

leek flamiche with
<u>CHEESE PASTRY</u>

60 g (2 oz) butter

4 leeks, white and pale green parts only, washed well, then thinly sliced

2 tablespoons dry white wine

pinch of sea salt flakes

300 g (10½ oz) crème fraîche or light sour cream

2 large free-range eggs

2 large free-range egg yolks

pinch of freshly grated nutmeg

CHEESE PASTRY

240 g (8½ oz/scant 1⅔ cups) plain (all-purpose) flour, plus extra for dusting

125 g (4½ oz) cold butter, cut into 5 mm (¼ inch) cubes

60 g (2 oz/½ cup) finely grated gruyère

2–3 tablespoons chilled water

melted butter, for brushing

To make the pastry, sift the flour onto a clean work surface. Toss the butter and cheese in the flour, then rub them in lightly until the mixture resembles very large flaky breadcrumbs. Make a well in the centre and pour in the water. Combine the mixture into a rough paste. Use the back of your hand to smear the pastry away from you, to further combine the butter and cheese with the flour. Knead until smooth.

Gather the pastry together and form into a flat disc shape. Wrap in plastic wrap and refrigerate for 20 minutes.

Roll the pastry out to a 5 mm (¼ inch) thickness. Brush a 22 cm (8¾ inch) deep fluted tart (flan) tin with melted butter. Use the rolling pin to lift the pastry onto the tart tin, then press it gently into the edge and the flutes of the tin, allowing the pastry a little extra height up the side as it will shrink during baking.

Chill the pastry in the tin for 20 minutes. Meanwhile, preheat the oven to 180°C/350°F (fan-forced).

Carefully line the pastry with baking paper and fill with baking beads, dried beans or rice. Bake for 15 minutes, then carefully remove the baking paper and weights and bake for a further 5 minutes. Remove from the oven and set aside.

To make the filling, melt the butter in a saucepan over low heat. Add the leek, then cover and cook, stirring occasionally, for 10 minutes. Stir in the wine and salt, cover and cook for a further 10 minutes, stirring occasionally. Remove the lid and continue cooking for a few more minutes, until the liquid has evaporated. Set aside to cool.

In a mixing bowl, combine the crème fraîche, eggs, egg yolks, nutmeg and cooled leek. Pour the mixture into the pastry case and smooth the top with a spatula. Bake for 40 minutes, or until the pastry top is golden and the centre is set.

The flamiche can be served warm, or can be refrigerated overnight in an airtight container and served at room temperature the following day. It is delicious with a peppery watercress salad.

Serves 6

NOTE
Flamiche is a specialty of
Picardy in northern France
and is best enjoyed with a
glass of Burgundy wine.

roast Provençal
__CHICKEN__

1.8 kg (4 lb) whole free-range chicken

1 lemon, cut in half

2 garlic cloves, crushed

2 teaspoons finely chopped rosemary

2 teaspoons finely chopped oregano

1 teaspoon chopped thyme

1 tablespoon melted butter

1 tablespoon olive oil

Preheat the oven to 220°C/430°F (fan-forced).

Rub the skin of the chicken with the cut sides of the lemon. Combine the remaining ingredients in a small bowl and season with sea salt and freshly ground black pepper. Massage the chicken inside and out with the mixture. Place the lemon halves inside the cavity.

Place the chicken on a wire rack in a roasting tin. Roast for 30 minutes, or until the skin begins to brown, then reduce the oven temperature to 180°C/350°F (fan-forced) and continue roasting for a further 30 minutes, or until the skin is golden brown and the juices run clear when a skewer is inserted into the thickest part of the thigh.

Remove from the oven and leave to rest for at least 10 minutes before carving — or leave whole, allow to cool, then wrap in foil and refrigerate until needed.

Serve with French potato salad (see page 71) or Pickled red onion & French lentil salad (see page 79).

Serves 4

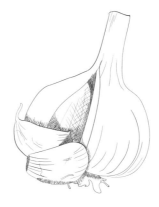

roast beef picnic
BAGUETTE WITH DUXELLES

40 g (1½ oz/¼ cup) pine nuts

1 sourdough baguette

6 thin slices of rare roast beef (from a delicatessen)

2 handfuls rocket (arugula) leaves

DUXELLES

40 g (1½ oz) butter

40 g (1½ oz/¼ cup) finely chopped French shallots

1 garlic clove, crushed

500 g (1 lb 2 oz) brown mushrooms, ends trimmed, finely chopped

60 ml (2 fl oz/¼ cup) white wine

1 tablespoon finely chopped flat-leaf (Italian) parsley

To make the duxelles, melt the butter in a large frying pan over medium heat. Add the shallot and garlic and cook, stirring, for about 3–4 minutes until softened. Add the mushrooms and season with sea salt and freshly ground black pepper. Cook, stirring, for about 10 minutes.

Stir in the wine, then cover and cook, stirring now and then, for 15 minutes, or until the liquid has evaporated and the mushrooms have the consistency of a paste. Stir the parsley through and allow to cool before using.

To toast the pine nuts, heat a small dry frying pan over medium heat. Add the pine nuts to the hot pan and cook, shaking the pan occasionally to turn them, for about 4 minutes, or until the nuts become golden. Remove from the pan to cool.

To assemble the baguette, slice it in half lengthways. Fold the roast beef slices onto the base, then pile on the rocket leaves and toasted pine nuts. Spread the inside of the lid with the duxelles and press the baguette halves together.

Cut the baguette into four or six portions. Wrap each one in greaseproof paper or baking paper, then tie with kitchen string or raffia.

Keep in the fridge and transport to your picnic destination in a chilled container. The baguettes are best enjoyed on the day of making.

Serves 4–6

NOTE
'Duxelles' is a French term, which refers to a sautéed mixture of mushrooms, onions, herbs and butter.

comté &
ASPARAGUS TART

250 ml (8½ fl oz/1 cup) thick (double/heavy) cream

3 free-range eggs, beaten

1 teaspoon dijon mustard

50 g (1¾ oz) comté or strong cheddar-style cheese, finely grated

pinch of sea salt flakes

2 bunches asparagus, or about 24 asparagus spears, base ends trimmed

PASTRY

225 g (8 oz/1½ cups) plain (all-purpose) flour, plus extra for dusting

120 g (4½ oz) cold butter, cut into 5 mm (¼ inch) cubes

1 free-range egg yolk, mixed with 1 teaspoon cold water

melted butter, for brushing

To make the pastry, sift the flour onto a clean work surface. Toss the butter cubes in the flour, then rub in lightly; small pieces of butter may still be visible. Make a well in the centre and pour in the egg yolk. Combine to form a smooth dough, then knead briefly until smooth.

Gather the dough together and form into a thick, flat disc. Wrap in plastic wrap and refrigerate for 30 minutes.

Brush a 35 cm x 12 cm (14 inch x 4¾ inch) tart (flan) tin with melted butter.

Dust your work surfact with flour, then roll out the pastry in the required shape, to a 5 mm (¼ inch) thickness. Use it to line the tart tin, allowing a little extra height up the sides, as the pastry will shrink during baking.

Chill the pastry in the fridge for 20 minutes. Meanwhile, preheat the oven to 180°C/350°F (fan-forced).

Line the chilled pastry with baking paper and fill with baking beads, dried beans or rice. Bake for 15 minutes, then remove the paper and weights and bake for a further 5 minutes. Remove from the oven and reduce the temperature to 160°C/320°F (fan-forced).

In a mixing bowl, whisk together the cream, eggs, mustard, cheese and salt until well combined.

Place the asparagus in a heatproof bowl, cover with boiling water and leave to blanch for 20 seconds, then drain and rinse briefly under cold running water. Drain well, then add to the cream mixture.

Pour the mixture into the pastry case and bake for 45 minutes, or until the filling is slightly golden on top and just set. Remove from the oven and leave to cool in the tin. Serve warm, or at room temperature.

The tart may be safely transported in the tin, wrapped in a clean linen cloth, and sliced and served on location. It is best enjoyed on the day of making, but can be refrigerated in an airtight container overnight and served at ambient temperature the following day.

Serves 4–6

spinach &
GRUYÈRE QUICHE

30 g (1 oz) butter

1 leek, pale part only, sliced

1 garlic clove, crushed

1 bunch English spinach, leaves trimmed and shredded; you'll need 200 g (7 oz) leaves

2 teaspoons thyme leaves

4 extra-large free-range eggs

250 ml (8½ fl oz/1 cup) thickened (whipping) cream

pinch of freshly grated nutmeg

165 g (6 oz/1¼ cups) grated gruyère

PASTRY

250 g (9 oz/1⅔ cups) plain (all-purpose) flour, plus extra for dusting

1 teaspoon sea salt

150 g (5½ oz) butter, softened

1 extra-large free-range egg

1 tablespoon cold milk

To make the pastry, combine the flour and salt on a work surface or in a large shallow bowl. Make a well in the centre. In the well, blend the butter and egg together, then gradually add in the flour from the edges, until the mixture looks like large crumbly breadcrumbs. Add the milk and mix to a dough, kneading four or five times until smooth.

Gently roll the pastry out between two sheets of baking paper, topped with a sprinkling of flour, to fit a rectangular 35 cm x 12 cm (14 inch x 4¾ inch) loose-based tart (flan) tin. Press the pastry in gently and prick the base a few times with a fork. Chill the pastry in the fridge for 1 hour.

Preheat the oven to 180°C/350°F (fan-forced). Cover the pastry with baking paper and fill with baking beads, dried beans or rice. Bake for 15 minutes.

Turn the oven down to 160°C/320°F (fan-forced). Carefully remove the paper and weights, then bake for a further 15 minutes, or until pale golden. Remove from the oven and leave to cool while preparing the filling.

Reduce the oven temperature to 140°C/275°F (fan-forced).

Melt the butter in a frying pan over medium heat. Add the leek and cook for 2 minutes. Add the garlic, spinach and thyme and cook for 3–4 minutes, until the spinach has wilted and any liquid has evaporated. Season with sea salt and freshly ground black pepper. Remove to a bowl to cool.

In a large bowl, whisk the eggs, cream and nutmeg together. Add the cooled spinach mixture and about 130 g (4½ oz/1 cup) of the gruyère.

Place the tart tin on a baking tray and gently fill the pastry case with the spinach mixture, being careful it doesn't run over the sides. Sprinkle with the remaining gruyère.

Bake for 35 minutes, or until the filling has set. Allow to cool slightly before gently removing from the tin.

This quiche is lovely served still a little warm, but is also good cold. If serving cold, cut into slices, keep chilled in an airtight container, and use within 2 days.

Serves 6–8

potato &
PUMPKIN TOURTE

20 g (¾ oz) butter

100 g (3½ oz) jambon or smoked ham, chopped

8 French shallots, thinly sliced

2 garlic cloves, crushed

400 g (14 oz) crème fraîche or light sour cream

1 tablespoon finely chopped flat-leaf (Italian) parsley

1 tablespoon finely chopped chives

1 tablespoon finely chopped tarragon

800 g (1 lb 12 oz) boiling (waxy) potatoes, such as bintje or Dutch cream, peeled and thinly sliced

400 g (14 oz) pumpkin (winter squash), peeled and thinly sliced

ROUGH PUFF PASTRY

300 g (10½ oz/2 cups) plain (all-purpose) flour

300 g (10½ oz) cold butter, cut into 5 mm (¼ inch) cubes

150 ml (5 fl oz) chilled water

melted butter, for brushing

1 free-range egg, beaten

To make the pastry, sift the flour onto a clean work surface and make a well in the centre. Use a pastry scraper to 'cut' the butter into the flour. Make a well in the middle and pour in the cold water. Using the pastry scraper, work the flour and butter into the water until the mixture holds together; small pieces of butter will still be visible. Flour your work surface, then roll the pastry out into a 15 cm x 40 cm (6 inch x 16 inch) rectangle. Fold both ends into the centre, then fold in half again, as though closing a book. Cover with plastic wrap and rest in the fridge for 20 minutes. Repeat the rolling, folding and resting steps twice more. Wrap in plastic wrap and rest for a further 30 minutes before using.

Preheat the oven to 160°C/320°F (fan-forced). Melt the butter in a saucepan over medium heat. Add the ham and cook for 3–4 minutes, stirring occasionally. Add the shallot and garlic and cook, stirring, for 4–5 minutes, until the shallot has softened.

In a bowl, combine the crème fraîche, parsley, chives and tarragon. Season generously with sea salt and freshly ground black pepper.

Cut one-third of the pastry from the block. Roll it out into a rectangle, slightly smaller than 20 cm x 30 cm (8 inches x 12 inches). Set aside. Roll out the remaining pastry into a larger rectangle, slightly smaller than 30 cm x 40 cm (12 inches x 16 inches).

Brush a deep rectangular baking tin, measuring about 20 cm x 30 cm x 3 cm (8 inches x 12 inches x 1¼ inches), with melted butter. Line the tin with the larger pastry rectangle. Arrange one-third of the potato and pumpkin slices over the pastry base. Scatter with half the ham mixture, then spread half the crème fraîche mixture over the top. Repeat the layering, finishing with slices of potato and pumpkin. Place the remaining pastry sheet on top and brush with the beaten egg. Fold in the edges, then use a small knife to create steam vents in the top of the pastry. Bake for 1½ hours, or until the pastry is deep golden brown, and the potato is tender when pierced with a skewer.

The tourte will travel well in the baking tin, wrapped in a clean linen cloth.

Serves 6–8

croque
MONSIEUR

8 slices of sourdough bread (see Note), about 1.5 cm (½ inch) thick

40 g (1½ oz) butter, softened

3 tablespoons dijon mustard

200 g (7 oz) good-quality sliced leg ham

60 g (2 oz/½ cup) grated gruyère

2 handfuls picked watercress or baby rocket (arugula) leaves (optional)

BÉCHAMEL SAUCE

15 g (½ oz) butter

1 tablespoon plain (all-purpose) flour

125 ml (4 fl oz/½ cup) milk

40 g (1½ oz/⅓ cup) grated gruyère

1 tablespoon finely chopped flat-leaf (Italian) parsley

freshly ground white pepper, to taste

To make the béchamel sauce, melt the butter in a small heavy-based saucepan over medium heat. Add the flour and stir to make a smooth paste. Cook, stirring, for 1 minute, or until bubbling and white, then gradually whisk in the milk until smooth. Simmer for a further 1–2 minutes, until thick.

Remove from the heat and stir in the gruyère until melted. Add the parsley, stir and season lightly with sea salt and freshly ground white pepper. Press a piece of baking paper over the surface of the sauce to stop a skin forming, then set aside.

Generously spread one side of each slice of bread with the butter; spread the other side with the mustard. Place 4 of the buttered slices in a large heavy-based frying pan, buttered side down, and top with the ham. Carefully spread the béchamel sauce over, then sprinkle with the gruyère. Finish with the remaining bread, mustard side uppermost.

Place the pan over medium–low heat and cook the sandwiches, turning occasionally, for about 15 minutes, or until the bread is deep golden and very crispy, and the cheese inside has melted.

If you are leaving for your picnic immediately and don't have too far to travel, wrap the toasted sandwiches securely in foil to keep them warm, or to enjoy cool, transfer from the frying pan to a wire rack to cool. Cut into fingers, then wrap each sandwich securely in baking paper for transportation.

Serve with a scattering of watercress or rocket, if desired.

Serves/makes 4

NOTE
You can cut the crusts from the bread, if you like. But leaving them on will give the sandwiches slightly chewy – and delicious – edges.

NOTE
You can buy capsicums already roasted, but it's easy to roast your own if you have time. To roast capsicums, place them directly on a gas burner, turning regularly with tongs until blackened on all sides. Place the capsicums in a plastic bag or wrap in foil and let them steam for 5–10 minutes. When cool enough to handle, peel away the blackened skin and remove the seeds and membranes. If you don't have a gas hob, you can bake them in a hot oven for about 30 minutes, or slice them in half, place them skin side up under a hot grill (broiler) and leave them until blackened.

basil, goat's cheese &
<u>TAPENADE BÂTARD</u>

2 bâtards (short baguettes), each about 25–27 cm (10–10¾ inches) long

12 basil leaves

4 roasted red capsicums (bell peppers), peeled, seeded and cut into strips (see Note)

100 g (3½ oz) goat's cheese, sliced

TAPENADE
155 g (5½ oz/1 cup) pitted kalamata olives

3 anchovy fillets, drained

1 tablespoon baby capers, drained and rinsed

1 tablespoon flat-leaf (Italian) parsley

2 teaspoons lemon juice

60 ml (2 fl oz/¼ cup) extra virgin olive oil

Put the tapenade ingredients in a small food processor and blend together to form a paste.

Cut each bâtard in half horizontally, but not all the way through. Spread the cut surfaces of the bread with the tapenade. (Store any leftover tapenade in the fridge in an airtight container, where it will keep for up to 2 weeks.)

On the bottom half of each bâtard, arrange six basil leaves, half the capsicum strips and half the goat's cheese. Close the lids back over.

Slice each loaf in half diagonally, and wrap in serviettes or napkins to serve, or slice into smaller pieces if you prefer. They are best enjoyed the day they are made.

Serves 4

pan bagnat
PICNIC SANDWICH

1 x 20 cm (8 inch) round rustic bread loaf

2 tablespoons olive oil

2 teaspoons apple cider vinegar

2 anchovy fillets, chopped

½ small red onion, finely chopped

2 free-range eggs, hard-boiled, peeled and sliced

180 g (6½ oz) tin of tuna packed in olive oil, drained

40 g (1½ oz/⅓ cup) pitted black olives, roughly chopped

1 red capsicum (bell pepper), thinly sliced

2 tomatoes, thickly sliced

1 Lebanese (short) cucumber, thinly sliced

Use a serrated knife to cut the loaf horizontally, all the way through; it helps to make the base larger than the top. Remove a little of the inside of the bread, to create a cavity. Sprinkle both cut sides of the loaf with the olive oil and vinegar.

Scatter the anchovy fillets evenly over the base of the loaf, then top with the onion and egg slices.

In a small bowl, break up the tuna chunks with a fork. Add the olives and capsicum and stir to combine. Spread the tuna mixture over the egg slices. Lay the tomato slices over the top and sprinkle with sea salt and freshly ground black pepper. Add the cucumber slices, then place the bread lid on top.

Press the loaf back together again firmly, then wrap tightly with plastic wrap. Place on a tray or cutting board, and place another tray or board on top and press down for a few minutes, or place some tins of food on top to compress the loaf.

Refrigerate for at least 4 hours, and up to 8 hours.

Unwrap and slice into six wedges to serve.

Serves 6

NOTE
You can use the Herb &
roasted garlic goat's cheese
from page 29 if you like.

goat's cheese &
__TOMATO GALETTES__

2 sheets (about 370 g/13 oz) frozen butter puff pastry

2 tablespoons olive oil

350 g (12½ oz) mixed vine-ripened cherry tomatoes

1 red onion, cut into thin wedges

1 teaspoon caster (superfine) sugar

25 g (1 oz/⅓ cup) fresh sourdough breadcrumbs

200 g (7 oz) soft goat's cheese (see Note)

2 handfuls rocket (arugula) leaves

Preheat the oven to 200°C/400°F (fan-forced). Line two baking trays with baking paper.

Allow the pastry to partially thaw, then place on the baking trays. Without cutting all the way through, use a small sharp knife to cut a border about 1 cm (½ inch) in from the edge of the pastry. Prick the centre area of each pastry sheet lightly with a fork.

Heat the olive oil in a frying pan. Add the tomatoes, onion and sugar and cook over medium heat, shaking the pan occasionally, for about 3–4 minutes, or until the tomatoes are shiny and the skins begin to split. Drain on paper towel.

Sprinkle the breadcrumbs over the pastry sheets, inside the border. Top with the tomato mixture, crumble the goat's cheese over and season with sea salt and freshly ground black pepper. Bake for 15–20 minutes, or until the pastry is puffed, well browned and cooked through.

Remove from the oven and cool the galettes on wire racks. Serve topped with the rocket.

The galettes are best enjoyed the day they are made.

Serves 4

La SALADE

salade
LYONNAISE

4 large free-range eggs

200 g (7 oz) smoked bacon, thickly sliced, then cut into 2 cm (¾ inch) long sticks

1 French shallot, finely chopped

1 tablespoon lemon juice

1 teaspoon dijon mustard

2 tablespoons extra virgin olive oil

1 frisée or curly endive lettuce (or other bitter or peppery greens, such as mâche, lamb's lettuce, mizuna, cress or rocket/arugula), washed and torn

Place the eggs in a small saucepan and cover with cold water. Put the lid on and place over high heat. Bring the water to the boil, then remove from the heat and stand, covered, for 6 minutes. Drain the water, then cover the eggs with cold water to stop them cooking further.

Heat a small frying pan over medium heat. Add the bacon and 250 ml (8½ fl oz/1 cup) water. Cook for 15–20 minutes, until the water has evaporated and the bacon is crisp. Add the shallot and cook for a further minute or two, until softened. Drain the mixture on paper towel and leave to cool before packing into a small airtight container.

To make the dressing, combine the lemon juice, mustard and 1 tablespoon water in a small mixing bowl. Season with sea salt and freshly ground black pepper. Add the olive oil in a thin stream, while whisking to emulsify. Transfer the dressing to a small jar with a screw-top lid for safe transport.

To assemble the salad, place the frisée leaves in a salad bowl. Add the bacon and shallot, pour the dressing over and toss gently to coat the leaves. Serve as a nest on individual plates or bowls, and invite each diner to break their egg as they add it to their salad.

Serves 4

NOTE
This salad is best assembled at the picnic location. The eggs can be peeled in advance and transported safely in a sealed container, or peeled by each diner and added to their salad. The broken yolk will add a richness to the dressing of the salad.

roasted beetroot,
ORANGE & DUCK SALAD

8 baby beetroot (beets),
washed well, top leaves
trimmed

2 tablespoons olive oil

2 duck breasts

1 curly endive, washed

2 handfuls picked watercress
sprigs

1 blood orange, peeled
and cut between the
membranes, into segments

VINAIGRETTE

½ teaspoon orange zest

½ teaspoon dijon mustard

2 teaspoons white wine
vinegar

1 tablespoon olive oil

Preheat the oven to 200°C/400°F (fan-forced).

Place the beetroot in a small ovenproof dish, drizzle with the olive oil and sprinkle with sea salt. Add 125 ml (4 fl oz/½ cup) water to the dish and roast for 30–35 minutes, or until the beetroot is tender. Leave to cool, then peel and cut into quarters.

Increase the oven temperature to 220°C/430°F (fan-forced). Season the duck breasts with sea salt and freshly ground black pepper.

Heat a frying pan over high heat. Add the duck breasts, skin side down, and cook for 4 minutes, or until the skin is brown. Turn them over and cook for a further 2 minutes.

Transfer the duck breasts to a baking tray lined with baking paper. Roast for 10 minutes. Remove from the oven and leave to rest for 10 minutes, then slice thinly.

In a bowl, whisk together the vinaigrette ingredients until well combined. Transfer to a small screw-top jar for safe transport.

Pack the duck, beetroot and salad ingredients separately, and chill until required.

At your picnic location, place the endive, watercress and orange segments in a salad bowl. Add the beetroot and duck and any roasting juices. Drizzle the dressing over and toss gently to combine. Serve at room temperature.

Serves 4–6

celeriac
REMOULADE

1 small celeriac, about 500 g (1 lb 2 oz)

1 teaspoon salt (optional)

2 teaspoons lemon juice (optional)

1 tablespoon roughly chopped herbs, such as flat-leaf (Italian) parsley, chervil or chives

REMOULADE

185 g (6½ oz/¾ cup) homemade or good-quality mayonnaise

2 tablespoons dijon mustard

2 tablespoons lemon juice or white wine vinegar

freshly ground white pepper, to taste

Peel the celeriac, then cut into long thin julienne strips, either by hand, or using a mandoline if you have one. Taste the celeriac: if it's slightly bitter, toss it in a large bowl with the salt and lemon juice, set aside for 30 minutes, then rinse and dry well with paper towel.

Place the celeriac in a large bowl.

To make the remoulade, put the mayonnaise, mustard and lemon juice in a small bowl. Season with sea salt and freshly ground white pepper and whisk together.

Add the remoulade to the celeriac strips and toss to combine well. Cover and refrigerate for 2–3 hours, or overnight, for the celeriac to soften slightly.

This salad will keep in an airtight container in the fridge for up to 3 days. Serve sprinkled with the herbs.

This simple salad is excellent served with the Pistachio, lemon thyme & chicken terrine (see page 14), or the Roast Provençal chicken (see page 45).

Serves 4–6

NOTE
For a little extra, you could garnish the salad with sliced hard-boiled eggs, or mix in some sliced roasted red capsicum (bell pepper), thinly sliced red onion or sliced cornichons.

French
POTATO SALAD

1 kg (2 lb 3 oz) baby potatoes, halved

2 tablespoons chopped flat-leaf (Italian) parsley

1 tablespoon chopped chives

1 tablespoon chopped tarragon

1 tablespoon baby capers, drained and rinsed

DRESSING

1 French shallot, finely chopped

2 teaspoons dijon mustard

2 tablespoons Champagne vinegar or white wine vinegar

80 ml (2½ fl oz/⅓ cup) extra virgin olive oil

Place the potatoes in a large saucepan and cover with cold water. Add some salt, bring to the boil, then leave to boil for 15 minutes, or until just tender. Drain and allow to cool slightly.

Put all the dressing ingredients in a jug and whisk together well. Season with sea salt and freshly ground black pepper.

While the potatoes are still warm, gently toss the dressing through them, then stir the herbs and capers through. Season again.

Transfer to an airtight container for transporting.

This salad is best dressed near serving time, so all the dressing doesn't get absorbed. If making ahead of time, pack the potatoes and dressing separately and gently toss the dressing through just before serving.

Serves 4–6

salade
NIÇOISE

500 g (1 lb 2 oz) baby
  potatoes, halved

200 g (7 oz) green beans,
  trimmed

3 extra-large free-range eggs

425 g (15 oz) tin of tuna in
  spring water or oil, drained

100 g (3½ oz) cherry
  tomatoes, halved

80 g (2¾ oz/½ cup) pitted
  kalamata olives

50 g (1¾ oz) rocket (arugula)

handful flat-leaf (Italian)
  parsley

2 baby Lebanese (short)
  cucumbers, halved
  lengthways, or 1 small
  one, sliced

DRESSING

1 French shallot, finely
  chopped

1 small garlic clove, crushed

3 teaspoons dijon mustard

½ teaspoon sugar, or to
  taste

60 ml (2 fl oz/¼ cup) lemon
  juice

80 ml (2½ fl oz/⅓ cup) extra
  virgin olive oil

Place the potatoes in a large saucepan and cover with cold water. Add some salt, bring to the boil, then leave to boil for 10–15 minutes, or until just tender. During the last 1–2 minutes, add the beans to blanch them. Drain, then rinse briefly under cold water to stop the beans cooking any further.

Put the eggs in a saucepan, cover with cold water and bring to the boil. Reduce the heat and simmer for 5–7 minutes, depending on how firm you like your eggs. Drain and run under cold water. Leave until cool enough to handle, then peel and cut in half.

Combine the potatoes and beans in a large bowl, along with the tuna, cherry tomatoes, olives, rocket, parsley and cucumber.

In a jug, whisk the dressing ingredients together.

Drizzle the dressing over the salad, then stir it through. Season with sea salt and freshly ground black pepper, gently fold in the egg and serve.

Serves 6

NOTE
This salad is best dressed
just before serving, so if
making a few hours ahead,
pack the salad items,
egg halves and dressing
separately and gently toss
together at your picnic.

white bean salad
WITH FRESH HERBS

300 g (10½ oz/1½ cups) dried haricot, navy or cannellini beans

3 flat-leaf (Italian) parsley sprigs

2 thyme sprigs

1 bay leaf

2 garlic cloves, unpeeled

2 tablespoons white wine vinegar

60 ml (2 fl oz/¼ cup) olive oil

1 small red onion, finely diced

175 g (6 oz/1 cup) whole mixed olives

2 small tomatoes, diced

4 tablespoons finely chopped flat-leaf (Italian) parsley

25 g (1 oz/½ cup) basil leaves, torn

Place the beans in a saucepan, cover with plenty of cold water and bring to the boil. Reduce the heat and simmer for 10 minutes, then turn off the heat and leave to soak for 2 hours.

Drain the beans and cover with fresh water. Prepare a bouquet garni by tying the parsley, thyme and bay leaf together with unwaxed cooking twine. Add it to the beans with the garlic cloves. Bring to the boil, reduce the heat and simmer for 1½–2 hours, or until the beans are tender, and adding more water as required; dried beans vary greatly in cooking time, so keep an eye on them.

Drain the beans well, discard the bouquet garni and garlic, and place in a mixing bowl. While the beans are still warm, add the vinegar, olive oil and onion, season with sea salt and toss gently to combine. Leave to cool.

Stir the olives, tomato, parsley and basil through, then pack into an airtight container for transporting. Chill until required, but serve at room temperature.

Serves 4–6

witlof, blue cheese
& PEAR SALAD

100 g (3½ oz/1 cup) walnuts

1 corella or Williams pear

1 tablespoon lemon juice

200 g (7 oz) roquefort, gorgonzola or fragrant blue cheese

2 red witlof (chicory), leaves separated

¼ frisée or curly endive lettuce, leaves torn

DRESSING

1 garlic clove, crushed

¼ teaspoon sea salt flakes

1 teaspoon dijon mustard

1 tablespoon lemon juice

60 ml (2 fl oz/¼ cup) olive oil

Preheat the oven to 180°C/350°F (fan-forced).

Place the walnuts on a baking tray and bake for 5–10 minutes, or until fragrant. Remove the tray from the oven and leave to cool.

To make the dressing, add the garlic and salt to a mixing bowl. Using the back of a teaspoon, blend to a paste. Add the mustard and lemon juice and combine well, using a whisk. Whisk in the olive oil in a thin stream until the dressing thickens. Transfer to a small screw-top jar for safe transport. Pack the other ingredients separately.

This salad is best assembled at the picnic site, just before serving. Simply slice the pear thinly and toss in a salad bowl with the lemon juice. Crumble in the cheese and add the walnuts, witlof and frisée. Add the dressing and toss gently to coat the leaves in the dressing. Serve straight away.

Serves 4

NOTE
For added crunch, scatter
some toasted walnuts or pine
nuts over the salad.

pickled red onion &
FRENCH LENTIL SALAD

330 g (11½ oz/1½ cups) puy lentils or tiny blue-green lentils

2 fresh bay leaves

4 thyme sprigs

1 large carrot, finely diced

1 celery stalk, finely diced

30 g (1 oz/1 cup) chopped flat-leaf (Italian) parsley

2 tablespoons chopped dill

100 g (3½ oz) goat's cheese, crumbled

PICKLED RED ONION

1 red onion, very thinly sliced

250 ml (8½ fl oz/1 cup) red wine vinegar

1 tablespoon sea salt

1 tablespoon sugar

DRESSING

2 teaspoons dijon mustard

2 tablespoons red wine vinegar

80 ml (2½ fl oz/⅓ cup) extra virgin olive oil

To pickle the onion, place it in a bowl with the vinegar, salt and sugar. Mix together, cover and leave to pickle for at least 1 hour, or until soft. Drain well.

Add the lentils, bay leaves and thyme sprigs to a saucepan of unsalted water. Bring to the boil and cook at a rapid simmer for 15 minutes. Add the carrot and celery and cook for 7 minutes, or until the lentils and vegetables are tender. Drain and leave to cool.

Tip the lentil mixture into a large bowl. Add the parsley, dill and pickled onion.

In a jug, combine the dressing ingredients, whisking well. Pour it over the salad and mix through thoroughly. Season with sea salt and freshly ground black pepper. Serve scattered with the goat's cheese.

This salad can be made a day ahead, but is best dressed on the day of serving. The onion can also be pickled the day before serving.

Serves 6–8

SWEET DELIGHTS

lemon
MADELEINES

125 g (4½ oz) butter, plus
    extra for greasing

finely grated zest of 1 lemon

3 extra-large free-range
    eggs, at room temperature

110 g (4 oz/½ cup) sugar

pinch of sea salt

175 g (6 oz) plain
    (all-purpose) flour

1 teaspoon baking powder

LEMON GLAZE

110 g (4 oz) pure icing
    (confectioners') sugar,
    sifted

finely grated zest of 1 lemon

2 tablespoons lemon juice

Melt the butter in a saucepan and add the lemon zest. Set aside to cool slightly.

Using an electric mixer, beat the eggs, sugar and salt together for 5 minutes, or until thick and pale.

Sift the flour and baking powder over the top. Fold them through, then gently fold in the butter mixture until well combined. Cover and refrigerate the mixture for at least 1 hour, or preferably 4 hours or overnight.

Preheat the oven to 180°C/350°F (fan-forced). Generously grease a standard 12-hole madeleine tin with butter (or two madeleine tins, if you happen to have them).

Spoon the mixture into each greased madeleine cup, to about three-quarters full. Bake for 10–12 minutes, or until golden and puffed. Remove from the tin and cool for 5 minutes on a wire rack. If using only one madeleine tin, clean it out, butter it again, then cook the second batch in the same way.

For the lemon glaze, combine the icing sugar, lemon zest and juice in a small bowl. Add 1 tablespoon water and mix to a smooth glaze.

While they are still warm, dip the madeleines into the glaze to coat, then leave to cool on the wire rack. Place in an airtight container for transporting.

The madeleines, being a sponge mixture, are best eaten fresh the day they are made, so they don't dry out.

Makes 24

NOTE
To make lime madeleines, simply use lime zest and juice instead of lemon zest and juice. You could also omit the glaze and dust the madeleines with sifted icing (confectioners') sugar.

chocolate
<u>ÉCLAIRS</u>

1 free-range egg yolk, whisked with 4 teaspoons cold water

100 g (3½ oz) dark chocolate, roughly chopped, plus some shaved dark chocolate to garnish

50 g (1¾ oz) unsalted butter, roughly chopped

1 teaspoon glucose syrup

CRÈME PÂTISSIÈRE

375 ml (12½ fl oz/1½ cups) full-cream milk

1 vanilla bean, split in half lengthways, seeds scraped

55 g (2 oz/¼ cup) caster (superfine) sugar

1 free-range egg

1 free-range egg yolk

35 g (1¼ oz/¼ cup) plain (all-purpose) flour

finely grated zest of 1 lemon

80 ml (2½ fl oz/⅓ cup) thickened (whipping) cream (35% fat)

To make the crème pâtissière, combine the milk, vanilla bean pod and vanilla seeds in a small heavy-based saucepan over medium heat. Bring just to the boil, then remove from the heat. Meanwhile, in a heatproof bowl, beat the sugar, egg and egg yolk using an electric mixer, until thick and pale. Beat in the flour.

Remove the vanilla bean pod from the milk. While whisking, slowly pour the hot milk into the egg mixture and whisk until combined.

Return the mixture to the saucepan and cook, whisking constantly with a balloon whisk, for about 5 minutes, until the mixture thickens and comes to the boil. Remove from the heat and stir in the lemon zest.

Transfer to a bowl, cover the surface with plastic wrap and refrigerate for at least 2–3 hours, until well chilled. The crème pâtissière can be made 2–3 days in advance and kept in the fridge until required.

When you're ready to bake the éclairs, preheat the oven to 180°C/350°F (fan-forced). Line a baking tray with baking paper.

To make the choux pastry, place the butter and 125 ml (4 fl oz/½ cup) water in a small heavy-based saucepan over medium heat. Bring to the boil, add the flour and salt and stir with a wooden spoon for 1–2 minutes, until the mixture leaves the side of the pan and forms a ball.

Transfer the mixture to the bowl of an electric mixer and allow to cool for 2 minutes. Add the eggs one at a time, beating well after each addition. The finished pastry should be firm and glossy.

Transfer the choux mixture to a piping (icing) bag fitted with a 1 cm (½ inch) star nozzle. Pipe twelve 8 cm (3¼ inch) logs onto the lined baking tray, about 4 cm (1½ inches) apart. Neaten up any sticking-out bits with your finger dipped in a little water, then lightly brush the pastry with the beaten egg yolk. Splash a little water onto the baking tray to create steam when the pastry goes into the oven. Bake for 25 minutes.

CHOUX PASTRY

40 g (1½ oz) unsalted butter, chopped

75 g (2¾ oz/½ cup) plain (all-purpose) flour

pinch of sea salt flakes

2 free-range eggs

Reduce the oven temperature to 160°C/320°F (fan-forced) and bake for a further 10–15 minutes, or until the pastry is puffed, deep golden and firm. Remove from the oven and poke a small hole in each end of each pastry, to allow steam to escape. Cool on a wire rack.

Just before using, whisk the chilled crème pâtissière until smooth. Beat the cream until soft peaks form, then fold into the crème pâtissière in two batches. Transfer to a piping bag fitted with a 5 mm (¼ inch) plain nozzle. Insert the nozzle carefully into the steam holes in the pastries and fill with crème pâtissière from each end. Do not overfill.

Fill a small saucepan one-third full of water and bring to a simmer. Place the chocolate, butter and glucose syrup in a heatproof bowl, set it over the pan and stir until the chocolate has melted and the mixture is well combined. Carefully dip one side of each éclair into the chocolate mixture, allowing the excess to drip off.

Scatter with shaved chocolate, then leave to set for a few minutes.

Transfer to an airtight container and keep refrigerated until you depart for your picnic. The éclairs are best enjoyed the day they are made.

Makes 6

NOTE
The cooled choux pastry puffs could be made a day ahead, kept in an airtight container at room temperature, and filled and decorated just before departing for your picnic.

lemon &
ALMOND TART

1½ lemons

80 g (2¾ oz/⅓ cup) caster (superfine) sugar

2 free-range eggs

80 g (2¾ oz/¾ cup) almond meal

⅛ teaspoon pure almond extract

2 tablespoons flaked almonds

icing (confectioners') sugar, for dusting

thick (double/heavy) cream, to serve

PÂTE SUCRÉE (SWEET PASTRY)

150 g (5½ oz/1 cup) plain (all-purpose) flour, plus extra for dusting

55 g (2 oz/¼ cup) caster (superfine) sugar

60 g (2 oz) cold unsalted butter, chopped

2 free-range egg yolks

1 tablespoon iced water, approximately

To make the pâte sucrée, place the flour, sugar and butter in a food processor and pulse until the mixture resembles breadcrumbs. Add the egg yolks and iced water and process until the ingredients just come together, adding a little more iced water if necessary. Press the dough into a flat disc shape, cover with plastic wrap and refrigerate for 30 minutes.

Roll out the pastry between two sheets of lightly floured baking paper to about 3 mm (⅛ inch) thick, large enough to line a 20 cm (8 inch) loose-based tart (flan) tin. Ease the pastry into the tin, gently pressing it into the side, then trim the edge. Refrigerate for a further 30 minutes.

Meanwhile, preheat the oven to 170°C/340°F (fan-forced).

Cover the pastry with baking paper and fill with baking beads, dried beans or rice. Place on a baking tray and bake for 10 minutes. Carefully remove the paper and weights and bake for a further 10 minutes, or until the pastry is cooked through and lightly browned. Set aside to cool.

Finely grate the zest of one of the lemons. Juice the lemons, then strain the juice and set aside.

Place the sugar and eggs in the bowl of an electric mixer and beat for about 5 minutes, until the mixture is very thick and pale yellow. Beat in the almond meal, almond extract and reserved lemon juice.

Place the cooled pastry case on a baking tray and place on an oven rack. Carefully pour the lemon mixture into the tart case, then sprinkle with the flaked almonds. Bake for 18–20 minutes, or until the pastry is lightly browned and the filling is just set.

Remove from the oven and allow to cool in the tin, resting on a wire rack.

Dust lightly with icing sugar.

Transfer to an airtight container and keep refrigerated until you depart for your picnic. The tart is best enjoyed the day it is made, served with thick cream.

Serves 6–8

orange & lavender
MINICAKES

2 large free-range eggs

100 ml (3½ fl oz) olive oil

zest of ½ orange

100 ml (3½ fl oz) orange juice

50 ml (1¾ fl oz) Cointreau or other orange liqueur

a few drops of lavender essence

200 g (7 oz/1⅓ cups) plain (all-purpose) flour

145 g (5 oz/⅔ cup) caster (superfine) sugar

1 teaspoon baking powder

pinch of sea salt flakes

melted butter, for brushing

ORANGE GLAZE

60 g (2 oz/½ cup) icing (confectioners') sugar

½ teaspoon orange zest

1 tablespoon orange juice

lavender flowers, to garnish (optional)

Preheat the oven to 160°C/320°F (fan-forced).

In a mixing bowl, lightly whisk together the eggs, olive oil, orange zest, orange juice, liqueur and lavender essence.

Place the flour, sugar, baking powder and salt in the bowl of an electric mixer. Using a paddle attachment, slowly blend together. With the motor running slowly, add the whisked egg mixture. When combined, beat on high for 3 minutes, scraping down the side of the bowl occasionally.

Brush the bases and sides of eight mini cake tins, or eight holes of a large muffin tin, with melted butter. Pour in the batter, dividing it evenly. If using cake tins, place them on a baking tray for safe handling.

Transfer to the oven and bake for 20 minutes, or until a skewer inserted into one of the cakes comes out clean. Remove from the oven (using the baking tray if using cake tins) and leave to stand for 10 minutes, before removing from the tins onto a wire rack.

To make the orange glaze, sift the icing sugar into a mixing bowl. Stir in the orange zest and juice. When the cakes are cool, use a spoon to drizzle the glaze over them. Garnish with lavender flowers, if desired.

Transfer to an airtight container for transporting. The cakes are best enjoyed the day they are made.

Makes 8

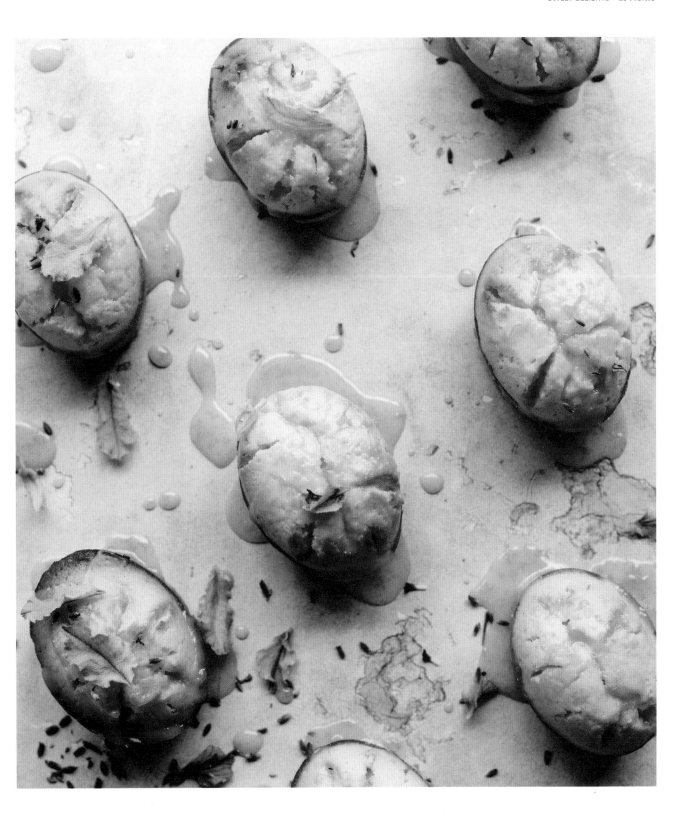

glazed fruit
TARTLETS

80 g (2¾ oz/¼ cup)
 raspberry jam

300 g (10½ oz) mixed
 berries and fruit, such as
 raspberries, blueberries,
 blackberries, grapes and
 cherries

ORANGE CRÈME
PÂTISSIÈRE

375 ml (12½ fl oz/1½ cups)
 full-cream milk

1 vanilla bean, split in half
 lengthways, seeds scraped

55 g (2 oz/¼ cup) caster
 (superfine) sugar

1 free-range egg

1 free-range egg yolk

35 g (1¼ oz/¼ cup) plain
 (all-purpose) flour

finely grated zest of 1 orange

1 tablespoon Cointreau
 or other orange liqueur
 (optional)

80 ml (2½ fl oz/⅓ cup)
 thickened (whipping)
 cream (35% fat)

To make the crème pâtissière, combine the milk, vanilla bean pod and vanilla seeds in a small heavy-based saucepan over medium heat. Bring just to the boil, then remove from the heat. Meanwhile, in a heatproof bowl, beat the sugar, egg and egg yolk using an electric mixer, until thick and pale. Beat in the flour.

Remove the vanilla bean pod from the milk. While whisking, slowly pour the hot milk into the egg mixture and whisk until combined.

Return the mixture to the saucepan and cook, whisking constantly with a balloon whisk, for about 5 minutes, until the mixture thickens and comes to the boil. Remove from the heat and stir in the orange zest and the liqueur, if using.

Transfer to a bowl, cover the surface with plastic wrap and refrigerate for at least 2–3 hours, until well chilled. The crème pâtissière can be made 2–3 days in advance and kept in the fridge until required.

To make the pâte sucrée, place the flour, sugar and butter in a food processor and pulse until the mixture resembles breadcrumbs. Add the egg yolks and iced water and process until the ingredients just come together, adding a little more iced water if necessary. Press the dough into a flat disc shape, cover with plastic wrap and refrigerate for 30 minutes.

Divide the pastry into six even portions. Roll out each pastry portion between two sheets of lightly floured baking paper to about 3 mm (⅛ inch) thick, large enough to line six 8 cm (3¼ inch) loose-based tart (flan) tins. Ease the pastry into the tins, gently pressing it into the sides, then trim the edges. Refrigerate for a further 30 minutes.

Meanwhile, preheat the oven to 170°C/340°F (fan-forced).

PÂTE SUCRÉE (SWEET PASTRY)

150 g (5½ oz/1 cup) plain (all-purpose) flour, plus extra for dusting

55 g (2 oz/¼ cup) caster (superfine) sugar

60 g (2 oz) cold unsalted butter, chopped

2 free-range egg yolks

1 tablespoon iced water, approximately

Cover the pastry with baking paper and fill with baking beads, dried beans or rice. Place the tins on a baking tray and bake for 10 minutes. Carefully remove the paper and weights and bake for a further 8–10 minutes, or until the pastry is cooked through and lightly browned. Set aside to cool.

Just before using, whisk the chilled crème pâtissière until smooth. Beat the cream until soft peaks form, then fold into the crème pâtissière in two batches. Refrigerate until required.

Heat the jam and 2 teaspoons water in a small saucepan over low heat until the jam has melted and the mixture has combined. Strain and discard the seeds.

Brush the insides of the cooled pastry cases with jam, then fill with the crème pâtissière. Arrange the fruit decoratively over the filling, pressing lightly into the crème. Brush the fruit lightly with the strained jam to glaze the tartlets.

Transfer to an airtight container and keep refrigerated until you depart for your picnic.

Makes 6

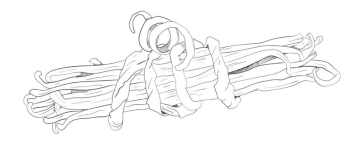

mini apple
GALETTES

3 granny smith apples

2 tablespoons thick (double/heavy) cream (minimum 45% fat)

2 sheets (about 370 g/13 oz) frozen butter puff pastry

2 teaspoons caster (superfine) sugar

3 tablespoons apricot jam

Preheat the oven to 210°C/410°F (fan-forced). Line two baking trays with baking paper.

Set one of the apples aside. Peel and core the remaining 2 apples, then roughly chop and place in a small saucepan with 60 ml (2 fl oz/¼ cup) water. Cover and cook over medium heat for 6–8 minutes, or until tender. Drain any excess liquid if necessary, transfer to a bowl, mash with a fork and set aside to cool. Stir in the cream.

Allow the pastry to partially thaw. Cut out eighteen 8 cm (3¼ inch) discs, placing them on the lined baking trays. Prick each pastry disc a few times with a fork, then refrigerate until required.

Core the remaining apple, cut it into quarters and very thinly slice lengthways, about 2 mm (¹⁄₁₀ inch) thick.

Spread 2 teaspoons of the cooled apple mixture over each pastry disc, leaving a 5 mm (¼ inch) border. Top each with three overlapping slices of apple and sprinkle with the caster sugar.

Bake for 10 minutes, then swap the baking trays around and bake for a further 8–10 minutes, or until the pastry is deep golden, cooked through and crisp, and the apple is browned; a few scorched spots are desirable. Transfer to wire racks to cool.

Meanwhile, heat the jam and 2 teaspoons water in a small saucepan over low heat, until the jam has melted and the mixture has combined. Strain and discard any pulp.

Brush the galettes lightly with the strained jam mixture to glaze.

Transfer to an airtight container and keep refrigerated until you depart for your picnic. The galettes are best enjoyed the day they are made.

Makes 18

strawberry
TART

80 g (2¾ oz/¼ cup)
strawberry jam

500 g (1 lb 2 oz)
strawberries, hulled
and cut in half

**LIQUEUR CRÈME
PÂTISSIÈRE**

375 ml (12½ fl oz/1½ cups)
full-cream milk

1 vanilla bean, split in half
lengthways, seeds scraped

55 g (2 oz/¼ cup) caster
(superfine) sugar

1 free-range egg

1 free-range egg yolk

35 g (1¼ oz/¼ cup) plain
(all-purpose) flour

2 tablespoons Framboise,
Cointreau or other orange
liqueur

80 ml (2½ fl oz/⅓ cup)
thickened (whipping)
cream (35% fat)

To make the crème pâtissière, combine the milk, vanilla bean pod and vanilla seeds in a small heavy-based saucepan over medium heat. Bring just to the boil, then remove from the heat. Meanwhile, in a heatproof bowl, beat the sugar, egg and egg yolk using an electric mixer, until thick and pale. Beat in the flour.

Remove the vanilla bean pod from the milk. While whisking, slowly pour the hot milk into the egg mixture and whisk until combined.

Return the mixture to the saucepan and cook, whisking constantly with a balloon whisk, for about 5 minutes, until the mixture thickens and comes to the boil. Remove from the heat and stir in the liqueur.

Transfer to a bowl, cover the surface with plastic wrap and refrigerate for at least 2–3 hours, until well chilled. The crème pâtissière can be made 2–3 days in advance and kept in the fridge until required.

To make the pâte sucrée, place the flour, sugar and butter in a food processor and pulse until the mixture resembles breadcrumbs. Add the egg yolks and iced water and process until the ingredients just come together, adding a little more iced water if necessary. Press the dough into a flat disc shape, cover with plastic wrap and refrigerate for 30 minutes.

Roll out the pastry between two sheets of lightly floured baking paper to about 3 mm (⅛ inch) thick, large enough to line a 23 cm (9 inch) loose-based tart (flan) tin. Ease the pastry into the tin, gently pressing it into the side, then trim the edge. Refrigerate for a further 30 minutes.

Meanwhile, preheat the oven to 170°C/340°F (fan-forced).

PÂTE SUCREE
(SWEET PASTRY)

150 g (5½ oz/1 cup) plain
   (all-purpose) flour

55 g (2 oz/¼ cup) caster
   (superfine) sugar

60 g (2 oz) cold unsalted
   butter, chopped

2 free-range egg yolks

1 tablespoon iced water,
   approximately

Cover the pastry with baking paper and fill with baking beads, dried beans or rice. Place on a baking tray and bake for 10 minutes. Carefully remove the paper and weights and bake for a further 10–12 minutes, or until the pastry is cooked through and lightly browned. Set aside to cool.

Just before using, whisk the chilled crème pâtissière until smooth. Beat the cream until soft peaks form, then fold into the crème pâtissière in two batches. Refrigerate until required.

Heat the jam and 2 teaspoons water in a small saucepan over low heat until the jam has melted and the mixture has combined. Strain and discard the seeds.

Brush the inside of the cooled pastry case with the jam, then fill with the crème pâtissière. Arrange the strawberries decoratively in concentric circles over the filling, pressing them lightly into the crème pâtissière.

Transfer to an airtight container and keep refrigerated until you depart for your picnic. This tart is best enjoyed the day it is made.

Serves 6–8

chocolate & Cointreau mousse
WITH PISTACHIO PRALINE

200 g (7 oz) dark chocolate (70% cocoa solids), roughly chopped

250 ml (8½ fl oz/1 cup) thickened (whipping) cream (35% fat), plus extra for serving

2 free-rage eggs, separated

finely grated zest of 1 orange

2 tablespoons Cointreau or other orange liqueur

1 tablespoon caster (superfine) sugar

250 g (9 oz) strawberries, hulled and chopped

PISTACHIO PRALINE

100 g (3½ oz/⅔ cup) pistachio nuts

115 g (4 oz/½ cup) caster (superfine) sugar

Fill a small saucepan one-third full of water and bring to a simmer. Place the chocolate and 60 ml (2 fl oz/¼ cup) of the cream in a heatproof bowl, then set it over the pan to melt the chocolate. Remove from the heat and set aside to cool slightly. Whisk in the egg yolks.

Beat the remaining cream until soft peaks form. Gently whisk the cream into the chocolate mixture, with the orange zest and liqueur.

In a clean bowl, beat the egg whites until frothy, using an electric mixer, then beat in the sugar. Beat until the mixture is glossy and soft peaks form. Fold into the mousse mixture until just combined, then pour into four 200 ml (7 fl oz) capacity serving dishes. Refrigerate for 1–2 hours, or until set; the mousse can easily be made a day ahead and refrigerated overnight.

To make the pistachio praline, spread the pistachios over a baking tray lined with baking paper, keeping them close together. Stir the sugar and 60 ml (2 fl oz/¼ cup) water in a small saucepan over low heat until the sugar dissolves. Increase the heat to medium and bring to the boil. Cook, without stirring, for 10 minutes, or until golden brown. Let the bubbles subside, then pour the mixture over the pistachios and set aside for 20 minutes, or until cold and set hard.

Break the praline into pieces and either leave in shards, or crush lightly using a mortar and pestle. Store in an airtight container until required.

Serve the chilled mousse topped with extra cream, praline and strawberries. It is best to transport the elements separately and simply assemble at the picnic, as the praline may melt or become sticky otherwise.

Serves 4

rose petal
TARTLETS

1 free-range egg

1 tablespoon caster (superfine) sugar

80 ml (2½ fl oz/⅓ cup) milk

80 ml (2½ fl oz/⅓ cup) thickened (whipping) cream (35% fat)

3 teaspoons rosewater

12 fresh unsprayed scented rose petals, or 2 tablespoons dried edible rose petals, plus extra to garnish

icing (confectioners') sugar, for dusting

ALMOND PASTRY

185 g (6½ oz/1¼ cups) plain (all-purpose) flour, plus extra for dusting

55 g (2 oz/¼ cup) caster (superfine) sugar

25 g (1 oz/¼ cup) almond meal

¼ teaspoon baking powder

90 g (3 oz) unsalted butter, chopped

1 free-range egg

2 teaspoons iced water, approximately

To make the pastry, place the flour, sugar, almond meal, baking powder and butter in a food processor and pulse until the mixture resembles breadcrumbs. Add the egg and iced water and process until the ingredients just come together, adding a little more water if necessary. Press the dough into a flat disc shape, cover with plastic wrap and refrigerate for 30 minutes.

Divide the pastry into six even portions. Roll out each pastry portion between two sheets of lightly floured baking paper to about 2–3 mm (1/16–1/8 inch) thick, large enough to line six 8 cm (3¼ inch) loose-based tart (flan) tins. Ease the pastry into the tins, gently pressing it into the sides, then trim the edges. Refrigerate for a further 30 minutes.

Meanwhile, preheat the oven to 170°C/340°F (fan-forced).

Cover the pastry with baking paper and fill with baking beads, dried beans or rice. Place the tins on a baking tray and bake for 10 minutes. Carefully remove the paper and weights and bake for a further 8–10 minutes, or until the pastry is cooked through and lightly browned. Set aside to cool.

Whisk the egg and sugar together in a jug until combined. Stir in the milk, cream and rosewater. Place 2 fresh rose petals or a teaspoon of dried rose petals in each pastry case. Fill with the cream mixture.

Bake for 15 minutes, then cover with foil and bake for a further 5 minutes, or until the custard is set.

Transfer to a wire rack to cool. Serve dusted with icing sugar and garnished with extra rose petals.

Transfer to an airtight container and keep refrigerated until you depart for your picnic. The tartlets are best enjoyed the day they are made.

Makes 6

raspberry
CLAFOUTIS

2 extra-large free-range eggs

115 g (4 oz/½ cup) caster (superfine) sugar

1 teaspoon vanilla paste or extract

50 g (1¾ oz/⅓ cup) plain (all-purpose) flour

250 ml (8½ fl oz/1 cup) thickened (whipping) cream

butter, for greasing

1 cup fresh (or unthawed frozen) raspberries

icing (confectioners') sugar, for dusting (optional)

In a small bowl, whisk together the eggs, caster sugar and vanilla. Add the flour, then the cream, and whisk until smooth. Allow the batter to rest for 30 minutes.

Meanwhile, preheat the oven to 170°C/340°F (fan-forced). Grease four mini gratin dishes, about 125 ml (4 fl oz/½ cup) capacity, with butter.

Divide the raspberries among the gratin dishes, then pour the batter over. Bake for 20–25 minutes, or until puffed and golden.

The clafoutis are best eaten warm, within a few hours of making, or can be chilled and eaten cold on your picnic. Dust with icing sugar before serving, if using.

Makes 4

La DRINK

tarragon
<u>LEMONADE</u>

230 g (8 oz/1 cup) caster (superfine) sugar

8 tarragon sprigs, leaves picked, plus extra to garnish

250 ml (8½ fl oz/1 cup) lemon juice; you'll need about 5 lemons

chilled soda water (club soda), to serve

lemon slices, to garnish

Combine the sugar and 125 ml (4 fl oz/½ cup) water in a small saucepan. Cook over medium heat, stirring, until the sugar has dissolved. Remove from the heat, stir in the tarragon leaves and lemon juice, then leave to cool to room temperature.

Remove the tarragon leaves and pour the cordial into a sterilised bottle with a tightly-fitting lid. Seal tightly and store in the fridge, where it will keep for up to 1 month.

To serve as a lemonade, simply combine 1 part cordial with 4 parts soda water. Garnish with extra tarragon sprigs and lemon slices.

Makes 450 ml (15 fl oz) cordial

NOTE
You could also add a dash of
the tarragon cordial to a tall
glass of cold black tea and
garnish with tarragon leaves.
Or pour a measure of gin over
ice, add a half measure of the
tarragon cordial and garnish
as described, or serve with a
cucumber stick as a stirrer.

NOTE
French 75 is a classic
cocktail made from gin,
Champagne, lemon juice and
sugar. Make it refreshing
and portable by packing the
French 75 syrup separately,
and adding the Champagne
and soda water at your
picnic destination. You can
make this in a punch bowl if
you prefer, to the proportions
of 3 parts Champagne,
2 parts syrup and 1 part soda
water, adding a little extra
soda water if you like.

French
75 SPRITZ

750 ml (25½ fl oz) bottle of Champagne or sparkling white wine, well chilled

chilled soda water (club soda), to serve

lemon zest strips or sliced lemon, to serve

FRENCH 75 SYRUP
55 g (2 oz/¼ cup) caster (superfine) sugar

110 ml (4 fl oz) lemon juice, strained

350 ml (12 fl oz) gin

To make the French 75 syrup, combine the sugar and lemon juice in a large jug. Stir for about 1 minute, until the sugar has dissolved. Add the gin, then pour into a sterilised bottle; you should end up with about 500 ml (17 fl oz/2 cups). Seal and refrigerate until required. The syrup will keep in the fridge for up to 2 weeks.

To serve, half-fill a Champagne flute with Champagne (or half-fill a wine glass with ice cubes, then half-fill with Champagne). Top two-thirds of the remaining space in the glass with French 75 syrup, and the final third with soda water.

Serve immediately, garnishing the glass with overhanging lemon zest strips, or adding some lemon slices to the glass.

Serves 8–10

calvados, Peychaud's
& APPLE PUNCH

ice cubes

1 red apple, thinly sliced into rings

handful mint leaves or sprigs

2 tablespoons Peychaud's Bitters (see Note)

60 ml (2 fl oz/¼ cup) lemon juice

100 ml (3½ fl oz) calvados (or brandy)

500 ml (17 fl oz/2 cups) apple cider

350 ml (12 fl oz) dry ginger ale, or to taste

Fill a large jug one-third full with ice cubes. Add the apple slices, mint, bitters, lemon juice and calvados, stirring gently to combine. Pour in the cider slowly, so it doesn't bubble up and spill over the top. Add ginger ale to taste, then serve.

Alternatively, this punch can be made in a punch bowl and served with a ladle, but that may not be as convenient for a picnic.

Serves 4–6

NOTE
Originally produced in
Louisiana, Peychaud's Bitters
is very red in colour and quite
sweet and spicy in taste.
You'll find it in specialist
bottle shops, or online.

champagne
COCKTAILS

Classic Champagne cocktail

1 sugar cube

3 drops of bitters

15 ml (½ fl oz) Cognac
   (optional)

chilled Champagne or
   sparkling white wine

a squeeze of lemon juice per
   glass, and/or a long strip
   of lemon peel with all the
   white pith removed

Place the sugar cube in a chilled Champagne glass. Add the bitters and allow
to soak in. Add the Cognac, if using, then top with Champagne. Add the lemon
and serve.

Serves 1

Rosewater & pomegranate Champagne cocktail

1 sugar cube

2 teaspoons rosewater

60 ml (2 fl oz/¼ cup) chilled
   pomegranate juice

chilled Champagne or
   sparkling white wine

Place the sugar cube in a chilled Champagne glass and add the rosewater.
Top with the pomegranate juice, then Champagne, and serve.

Serves 1

Chambord & orange Champagne cocktail

1 sugar cube

60 ml (2 fl oz/¼ cup) chilled blood orange juice

15–20 ml (½–¾ fl oz) Chambord (raspberry liqueur)

chilled Champagne or sparkling white wine

fresh raspberries or a thin slice of orange, to garnish

Place the sugar cube in a chilled Champagne glass. Add the orange juice and Chambord. Top with Champagne, garnish with raspberries or an orange slice and serve.

Serves 1

Champagne julep

1 sugar cube

2 mint sprigs

2 ice cubes

15–20 ml (½–¾ fl oz) crème de menthe or crème de cassis (optional)

chilled Champagne or sparkling white wine

Place the sugar cube in a chilled highball glass. Add the mint sprigs and ice cubes. Pour in the liqueur, if using. Top with Champagne and serve.

Serves 1

rosé
GRANITA

55 g (2 oz/¼ cup) caster (superfine) sugar

80 ml (2½ fl oz/⅓ cup) lemon juice

750 ml (25½ fl oz) bottle of rosé wine

In a large jug, combine the sugar, lemon juice and 125 ml (4 fl oz/½ cup) water. Stir for about 1 minute, until the sugar has dissolved. Pour into a shallow 1.25 litre (42 fl oz/5 cup) baking tin or container and add the wine. Stir to combine, then place in the freezer for 1½ hours, or until frozen around the edges.

Stir the granita to combine the frozen edges with the softer mixture in the centre. Freeze for a further 3–4 hours, or until frozen. Break up the mixture with a fork; it should form small ice crystals. The granita will keep in an airtight container in the freezer for up to 4 days.

Transport the granita to your picnic destination in a thermos or insulated flask, and it will remain frozen until ready to serve. Before spooning the granita into the flask, first pre-chill the flask by filling it with cold water and ice and letting it chill for 5 minutes. Discard the ice and water, carefully spoon the granita into the flask and seal tightly.

To serve, tip the granita into serving glasses and enjoy immediately. It will melt as you enjoy it, depending on the ambient temperature.

Serves 4

blackberry
FIZZ

500 g (1 lb 2 oz) fresh
blackberries

110 g (4 oz/½ cup) sugar

3–4 tarragon leaves, or
some dried lavender
(optional)

crushed or cubes of ice, to
serve

chilled soda water (club
soda) or ginger ale, to
serve

lemon or lime slices, to serve

Combine the blackberries and sugar in a saucepan. Pour in 125 ml (4 fl oz/½ cup) water and stir over low heat to dissolve the sugar, mashing the blackberries with a spatula or spoon.

Add the tarragon or lavender, if using. Bring to the boil, then reduce the heat and simmer for 3–4 minutes, until thickened and syrupy. Strain and leave to cool.

Pour the cold blackberry syrup into chilled glasses. Add ice, soda water and citrus slices then serve.

The blackberry syrup will keep in a clean airtight jar in the fridge for up to 2 weeks.

Serves 6–8

iced mint
__TISANE__

8 mint leaves, plus extra
   to garnish

4 lime slices

1 teaspoon sugar

ice cubes

chilled soda water (club
   soda)

Place the mint, lime slices and sugar in a heavy glass. Muddle until the mint leaves and lime slices are just bruised, to release their flavour. Add ice cubes, top up with soda water, garnish with extra mint leaves and serve.

Alternatively, you could put 8 mint leaves and 4 lime slices per person in a heatproof jug, pour boiling water over them, leave to infuse for about 10 minutes, then strain. Sweeten with 1 teaspoon sugar per person and chill in the fridge. Take chilled to your picnic destination, pour into glasses, top up with ice cubes and soda water, and serve garnished with extra mint leaves.

Serves 1

INDEX

Published in 2017 by Smith Street Books
Melbourne | Australia
smithstreetbooks.com

ISBN: 978-1-925418-29-3

CIP data is available from the National Library of Australia

Publisher: Paul McNally
Editor: Katri Hilden
Recipe development: Sue Herold, Jane O'Shannessy & Caroline Griffiths
Design concept: Michelle Mackintosh
Design layout: Heather Menzies, Studio31 Graphics
Photographer: Chris Middleton
Art Director & Stylist: Stephanie Stamatis
Home Economists: Caroline Griffiths & Jemima Good
Illustrator: Dave Adams

Printed & bound in China by C&C Offset Printing Co., Ltd.

Book 25
10 9 8 7 6 5 4 3 2 1